Crowdfunding Secrets: A Comprehensive Guide to Successfully Funding Your Next Project

B. Vincent

Published by RWG Publishing, 2023.

While every precaution has been taken in the preparation of this book, the publisher assumes no responsibility for errors or omissions, or for damages resulting from the use of the information contained herein.

CROWDFUNDING SECRETS: A COMPREHENSIVE GUIDE TO SUCCESSFULLY FUNDING YOUR NEXT PROJECT

First edition. April 18, 2023.

Copyright © 2023 B. Vincent.

Written by B. Vincent.

Also by B. Vincent

Affiliate Marketing
Affiliate Marketing
Affiliate Marketing

Standalone
Business Employee Discipline
Affiliate Recruiting
Business Layoffs & Firings
Business and Entrepreneur Guide
Business Remote Workforce
Career Transition
Project Management
Precision Targeting
Professional Development
Strategic Planning
Content Marketing
Imminent List Building
Getting Past GateKeepers
Banner Ads
Bookkeeping
Bridge Pages
Business Acquisition

Business Bogging
Business Communication Course
Marketing Automation
Better Meetings
Business Conflict Resolution
Business Culture Course
Conversion Optimization
Creative Solutions
Employee Recruitment
Startup Capital
Employee Incentives
Employee Mentoring
Followership
Servant Leadership
Human Resources
Team Building
Freelancing
Funnel Building
Geo Targeting
Goal Setting
Immanent List Building
Lead Generation
Leadership Course
Leadership Transition
Leadership vs Management
LinkedIn Ads
LinkedIn Marketing
Messenger Marketing
New Management
Newsfeed Ads
Search Ads
Online Learning
Sales Webinars

Side Hustles
Split Testing
Twitter Timeline Advertising
Earning Additional Income Through Side Hustles: Begin Earning Money Immediately
Making a Living Through Blogging: Earn Money Working From Home
Create Bonuses for Affiliate Marketing: Your Success Is Encompassed by Your Bonuses
Internet Marketing Success: The Most Effective Traffic-Driving Strategies
JV Recruiting: Joint Ventures Partnerships and Affiliates
Secrets to List Building
Step-by-Step Facebook Marketing: Discover How To Create A Strategy That Will Help You Grow Your Business
Banner Advertising: Traffic Can Be Boosted by Banner Ads
Affiliate Marketing
Improve Your Marketing Strategy with Internet Marketing
Outsourcing Helps You Save Time and Money
Choosing the Right Content and Marketing for Social Media
Make Products That Will Sell
Launching a Product for Affiliate Marketing
Pinterest as a Marketing Tool
Banner Blitz: Mastering the Art of Advertising with Eye-Catching Banners
Beyond Commissions: Maximizing Affiliate Profits with Creative Bonus Strategies
Retargeting Mastery: Winning Sales with Online Strategies
Power Partnerships: Mastering the Art of Business Growth Through Partnership Recruiting
The List Advantage: Unlocking the Power of List Building for Marketing Success
Capital Catalyst: The Essential Guide to Raising Funds for Your Business

Mobile Mastery: The Ultimate Guide to Successful Mobile Marketing Campaigns

Crowdfunding Secrets: A Comprehensive Guide to Successfully Funding Your Next Project

Table of Contents

Chapter 1: The Fundamentals of Crowdfunding: An Introduction 1

Chapter 2: The Psychology of Crowdfunding: Understanding Your Backers 5

Chapter 3: Choosing the Right Platform: Finding the Best Fit for Your Project 9

Chapter 4: Crafting a Compelling Crowdfunding Campaign: Tips and Tricks 13

Chapter 5: Creating a Killer Video: The Importance of Visual Storytelling 17

Chapter 6: Building Your Crowdfunding Team: Choosing the Right People for the Job 21

Chapter 7: The Power of Social Media: Maximizing Your Reach and Engagement 25

Chapter 8: Navigating Legal Issues: Crowdfunding Regulations and Compliance 29

Chapter 9: Rewards and Perks: Creating Incentives for Backers 33

Chapter 10: Setting Realistic Goals: Understanding Your Funding Needs 37

Chapter 11: Pre-Launch Strategies: Building Buzz and Anticipation .. 41

Chapter 12: Launch Day: Strategies for a Successful Campaign Launch 45

Chapter 13: Maintaining Momentum: Keeping Your Campaign Fresh and Engaging 49

Chapter 14: Engaging Your Backers: Staying Connected and Building Community.. 53

Chapter 15: Overcoming Obstacles: Common Challenges and How to Overcome Them... 57

Chapter 16: Managing Finances: Budgeting and Fulfillment Strategies.. 61

Chapter 17: The Aftermath: Post-Campaign Strategies for Success...... 65

Chapter 18: Going Global: Expanding Your Reach Beyond Your Borders... 69

Chapter 19: Success Stories: Inspiring Tales of Crowdfunding Triumph... 73

Chapter 20: The Future of Crowdfunding: Trends and Predictions for the Next Decade.. 77

Chapter 1: The Fundamentals of Crowdfunding: An Introduction

Crowdfunding has emerged as an effective method for generating financial support and bringing imaginative endeavors to fruition. The fundamentals of crowdfunding, such as its definition, the various forms it can take, and the advantages it can offer, will be discussed in this chapter.

Simply put, what is crowdsourcing?

The practice of raising money for a venture or project through the collection of numerous small contributions from a large number of people, most frequently through the use of the internet, is known as crowdsourcing or crowdfunding. It is a type of alternative finance that gives business owners, creatives, and individuals with an idea the ability to sidestep conventional sources of funding like banks, venture capitalists, and angel investors.

Different Variations of Crowdfunding

There are a few distinct models of crowdfunding, each of which has its own set of requirements and defining characteristics. The following are some of the most common types of crowdfunding:

Reward-based crowdfunding is a type of crowdfunding in which backers contribute funds in exchange for rewards or perks such as products, services, or exclusive experiences. Backers may receive these types of rewards in exchange for their contributions. It's common practice for creative endeavors like movies, albums of music, and video games to raise funds through this method of crowdsourcing.

Equity-based crowdfunding is a type of crowdfunding that allows backers to make investments in a company in exchange for ownership shares or equity in the company. This particular form of crowdfunding is very common among newly established companies and business owners who are looking to raise capital for their company.

Donation-based Crowdfunding: A type of crowdfunding in which backers contribute funds without any expectation of receiving a reward or equity in return is known as donation-based crowdfunding. This particular form of crowdfunding is very popular among charitable organizations, social causes, and relief efforts following natural disasters.

The Advantages of Participatory Financing

Crowdfunding is an option that entrepreneurs, creatives, and individuals with ideas should strongly consider using because it offers a number of benefits that make it an attractive choice. These advantages include the following:

Access to Capital: Crowdfunding makes it possible for creatives and entrepreneurs to access capital without having to rely on conventional sources of financing like banks or venture capitalists.

Crowdfunding can be a useful tool for determining whether or not there is a demand for a particular product or service in the market. Before devoting a significant amount of their time and resources to developing their concept, entrepreneurs can gauge the level of interest in and demand for their idea through the use of a crowdfunding campaign.

Constructing a Supporting Community Entrepreneurs can use crowdfunding to construct a community of backers who are invested in their idea and who are able to provide valuable feedback, support, and promotion of their endeavor.

Crowdfunding can be a cost-effective method of raising money for a project or business venture, depending on how it is structured. Crowdfunding, in contrast to traditional methods of obtaining financing, does not require business owners to make interest payments or give up equity in their company.

Conclusion

In conclusion, crowdfunding has become an effective tool that can be used to raise monetary support and bring imaginative projects to fruition. It is absolutely necessary for anyone who plans to launch a crowdfunding campaign to have a solid understanding of the basics of crowdfunding. In the following chapter, we will discuss the psychology of crowdfunding as well as how to understand the people who have supported your project.

Chapter 2: The Psychology of Crowdfunding: Understanding Your Backers

It is not only about raising money through crowdfunding; it is also about building a community of backers who believe in your idea and have an investment in your success. In this chapter, we will discuss the psychological aspects of crowdfunding and how to better understand the people who contribute to your project.

Why is It Necessary to Have a Good Understanding of Your Supporters?

It is absolutely necessary for the success of your crowdfunding campaign to have an understanding of your backers. You can tailor your campaign to appeal to your audience by first gaining an understanding of their motivations, desires, and expectations. This will allow you to build a stronger connection with your audience. This, in turn, can lead to higher levels of engagement, increased levels of support, and an increased likelihood of success.

Those Who Support It and Why

There are a variety of reasons that backers contribute financial support to crowdfunding campaigns. These are the following:

Backers may have a personal connection to the project or the creator, such as a shared interest or experience, which motivated them to contribute financially to the endeavor.

Belief in the Potential of the Idea Some backers may have faith in the capabilities of the idea and want to contribute to its further development.

Backers may be motivated by the promise of exclusive access to products, services, or experiences that are not available to the general public. This could be because backers desire to avoid missing out on these opportunities.

Motivated by altruism, backers may be driven to contribute to a project out of a desire to assist a social cause, charity, or community endeavor.

By gaining an understanding of these drivers, you can improve your ability to craft an engaging campaign that strikes a chord with your audience and motivates them to take action.

Characteristics of Supporters' Personalities

Although backers come from all walks of life, there are certain personality traits that are frequently associated with crowdfunding supporters. These are the following:

Early Adopters: Backers are frequently early adopters who have an interest in cutting-edge new products, services, and experiences. Backers can range from individuals to companies.

Backers are typically themselves creative and artistic individuals who have an appreciation for the work of other creatives and who are willing to support them financially.

Socially Conscious: Backers are typically socially conscious people who are concerned about social and environmental issues and who want to support causes that are congruent with their own personal beliefs and ideals.

Risk-Takers: Backers are often risk-takers who are willing to invest in unproven ideas and projects that have the potential for high returns. Backers are also willing to invest in unproven ideas and projects that have the potential for high returns.

By gaining an understanding of these characteristics, you can better tailor the messaging of your campaign and the rewards you offer to appeal to your audience and establish a more meaningful connection with your backers.

Emotional Triggers for Supporters of a Cause

Emotional triggers are highly effective motivators that can have a significant impact on the actions of your supporters. If you have an understanding of these triggers, you will be better equipped to craft an engaging campaign that will resound with your audience and motivate them to take action. Some of the most common emotional triggers experienced by backers are as follows:

Excitement Potential backers may be motivated to support a project because they are excited about the prospect of being a part of something original and cutting edge.

Empathy: Backers may be motivated to contribute because they feel a strong sense of empathy or compassion for the project's creator, the cause, or both.

Fear of Missing Out (FOMO): Backers may be motivated by the fear of missing out on exclusive rewards or experiences that are only available to backers of the project. These rewards and experiences are only available to backers.

Social Proof: It's possible that backers are inspired to support a campaign after seeing that other people are also supporting it and getting the sense that they are a part of a larger community.

Conclusion

In conclusion, knowing your supporters inside and out is absolutely necessary for running a successful crowdfunding campaign. You can tailor the messaging of your campaign and the rewards you offer to appeal to your audience by first gaining an understanding of their motivations, personality traits, and emotional triggers. This will allow you to build a stronger connection with your backers. In the following chapter, we will discuss how to select the most appropriate crowdfunding platform for your particular endeavor.

Chapter 3: Choosing the Right Platform: Finding the Best Fit for Your Project

It is absolutely essential to the success of your crowdfunding campaign that you select the appropriate platform. In this chapter, we will discuss the various types of crowdfunding platforms, as well as how to select the one that is going to be the most beneficial to your project.

Different kinds of platforms for crowdsourcing funding

There are a few distinct categories of crowdfunding platforms, each of which has its own set of requirements and defining characteristics. The following categories of crowdfunding platforms are the most common:

Platforms for General Crowdfunding: These platforms allow creators to launch campaigns for a wide variety of projects, including creative projects, social causes, and business ventures. Creators can raise funds for their projects on these platforms. GoFundMe, Indiegogo, and Kickstarter are some examples of crowdfunding platforms.

Platforms for equity crowdfunding: These platforms make it possible for startups and entrepreneurs to raise funds in exchange for ownership shares or equity in the company. SeedInvest, StartEngine, and Republic are a few examples of similar platforms.

Platforms for Crowdfunding that Are Based on Donations: These types of platforms make it possible for individuals and organizations to raise money for charitable causes, disaster relief, and other good causes. GlobalGiving, DonorsChoose, and Kiva are a few examples of such websites.

When Choosing a Platform, There Are Several Factors to Consider

When selecting a platform for crowdfunding, there are a number of considerations to make, including the following:

The type of project that you are going to launch is going to be the primary factor in determining the type of platform that you should go with. If you are starting a creative project, for instance, you might find that a general crowdfunding platform, such as Kickstarter or Indiegogo, is the most appropriate choice. If you are looking for funding for your startup business, an equity crowdfunding platform might be the best option for you to pursue.

Fees for the Platform Almost all crowdfunding platforms charge fees for the use of their services, which may include the processing of payments, the management of campaigns, and the provision of support. When selecting a platform, it is essential to take these fees into consideration because of the significant impact they can have on your overall fundraising objectives.

The audiences and user bases of the various crowdfunding platforms are distinctively distinct from one another. It is essential to select a medium that already has a user base that is compatible with the objectives of the project you are working on.

Requirements for Campaigns Different crowdfunding platforms have different requirements for launching campaigns, including minimum funding goals, campaign duration, and project categories. These requirements can be found in the campaign requirements section. It is essential to select a platform that is compatible with the requirements of your campaign.

Support and Resources: Depending on the platform, creators can receive varying degrees of support and access to a variety of resources. It is essential to select a platform that gives you access to the support and resources you require in order to launch a campaign that is successful.

Conclusion

It is absolutely essential to the success of your crowdfunding campaign that you select the appropriate platform. You can choose a platform that is the best fit for your project if you take into consideration the type of project you are working on, the platform fees, the audience, the campaign requirements, and the support and resources that are available. In the following chapter, we will discuss the various components that make up an effective crowdfunding campaign.

Chapter 4: Crafting a Compelling Crowdfunding Campaign: Tips and Tricks

It is essential to create a compelling crowdfunding campaign if you want to attract and keep the interest of backers. In this chapter, we will discuss a variety of helpful hints and pointers that can be utilized when developing a successful crowdfunding campaign.

Create a Pitch that Is Both Clear and Captivating

Your campaign pitch needs to communicate your idea, the benefits it offers, and the potential impact it could have in a way that is both clear and concise. It ought to be interesting to look at while also being simple to comprehend. Your presentation could be improved and made more interesting by incorporating visuals, videos, and other forms of media.

Establish Funding Objectives That Are Realistic

It is absolutely necessary to set funding goals that are attainable in order to have a successful crowdfunding campaign. Make sure that you take into account all of the costs that are associated with your project, and decide on a funding goal that is attainable. Think about estimating your costs with the help of a funding calculator so you can figure out how much money you need.

Make sure that the rewards and perks you offer are appealing as well as pertinent.

Providing backers with incentives in the form of rewards and perks is an excellent way to generate excitement for your campaign. Take care to develop rewards that are not only appealing but also pertinent to the project at hand and in line with its goals. You might think about providing early backers with exclusive merchandise, discounts, or even special access to your project.

Utilize Other Channels in Addition to Social Media for Promotional Purposes

Your campaign will not be successful without proper promotion. Make sure that you promote your campaign using social media as well as other channels so that you can reach a larger audience. You can increase your visibility and engagement by employing various strategies, such as hashtags and influencers.

Interact with Your Financial Supporters and Create a Thriving Community

It is essential to maintain communication with your backers if you want to build a strong community and generate support for your project over the long term. Be sure to engage with your backers by responding to their comments, providing updates, and including them in the process of developing your project. If you want to keep your backers interested and energized, you should think about hosting events, live streams, and other activities.

Maintain Open and Honest Communication Obviously and Remaining Consistently

It is imperative that you be transparent with your backers in order to earn their trust. Throughout the entirety of your campaign, you should make sure to communicate in a way that is both clear and consistent. You should provide regular updates and address any concerns or issues that may arise. Be truthful and open about the progress of your project as well as any obstacles or delays you may be experiencing.

Present both an engaging narrative and a compelling value proposition.

It is essential to have a compelling story as well as a solid value proposition in order to attract and engage potential backers. Make sure to tell a story that your audience can relate to and that effectively conveys the one-of-a-kind value that your project offers. Think about utilizing testimonies, case studies, or any number of other strategies to bolster your credibility and demonstrate the positive impact of your project.

Conclusion

It is essential to create a compelling crowdfunding campaign if you want to attract and keep the interest of backers. You can create a successful crowdfunding campaign by developing a pitch that is both clear and compelling, setting funding goals that are realistic, creating rewards and perks that are appealing, leveraging social media and other channels for promotion, engaging with your backers, being transparent and communicating clearly and consistently, offering a compelling story and a strong value proposition, and offering all of these things at the same time. In the following chapter, we will discuss the steps necessary to create a compelling video for your crowdfunding campaign.

Chapter 5: Creating a Killer Video: The Importance of Visual Storytelling

Video is a powerful tool that you can use to engage your audience and communicate the message you want to convey. In this chapter, we will discuss the significance of visual storytelling as well as the steps necessary to produce an eye-catching video for your crowdfunding campaign.

Why the Use of Video in Crowdfunding Campaigns is So Important

A crowdfunding campaign that is successful almost always includes some sort of video component. It gives you the opportunity to tell your story in a way that is compelling and engaging, to showcase your project, and to establish a connection with your audience. According to Kickstarter's data, campaigns that include videos have a success rate that is twenty percent higher than campaigns that do not include videos.

The Importance of Visual Narrative in Today's World

Telling a story through images is an effective method for getting your point across and establishing a rapport with the people you're speaking to. It includes telling a story through the use of visual elements, such as pictures and video, in order to elicit feelings. Visual storytelling can assist you in the following ways:

Make an Impression That Will Last: Visuals are more easily remembered than text, and they have the potential to make an impression on your audience that will last.

Evoke Emotions: Your audience will be able to connect with your message on a deeper level if you use visuals that are able to evoke emotions.

Communicate Complicated Concepts Through the use of visuals, which can help to simplify difficult concepts and make them simpler and easier to understand.

Show, Don't Tell: You can use visuals to demonstrate how your project will benefit your audience, rather than simply describing it to them verbally.

Instructions on How to Make a Viral Video

The production of a killer video calls for meticulous planning and precise execution. The following are some suggestions that will assist you in the production of a video that will captivate your audience and motivate them to contribute to your cause:

Because people have such short attention spans, it is important that your video be concise and get right to the point. Aim for a duration of two to three minutes.

Tell a Story: Your video should tell an engaging story that your audience can identify with and that will resonate with them. Keep in mind the impact that your project will have as well as the issue that it will solve.

Display Your Project Make use of visuals to display your project in order to provide your audience with a clear understanding of what it is that you are attempting to accomplish.

Exhibit Your Personality: The video you create should exhibit your personality and facilitate a more personal connection between you and the viewers of the video.

Make Sure to Use High-Quality Visuals and Audio in Your Video: Your video should be appealing to the eye and the ear. Create a video that has the appearance of professionalism by using audio and visual elements of a high quality.

Include a Call-to-Action: Your video ought to incorporate a distinct call-to-action that directs viewers to your crowdsourcing campaign.

Test and Improve: Show your video to a select few people, get their feedback, and then work to improve it based on what you learned from them. Check to see if it strikes a chord with the people you want to listen to it.

Conclusion

Making a compelling video is one of the most important steps in running a successful crowdfunding campaign. You can create a video that captivates your audience and encourages them to support your cause by recognizing the significance of visual storytelling, keeping your video succinct and to the point, telling a story that is compelling, showcasing your project, displaying your personality, making use of high-quality visuals and audio, including a call to action, and testing and refining your video. In the following chapter, we will discuss how to construct your crowdfunding team and select the most qualified candidates for the positions available.

Chapter 6: Building Your Crowdfunding Team: Choosing the Right People for the Job

It takes the combined efforts of a group of people to launch a successful crowdfunding campaign. In this chapter, we will discuss how to construct your crowdfunding team as well as how to select the appropriate individuals for the position.

Why It's Necessary for You to Have a Crowdfunding Team

Putting together a crowdsourcing team is one of the most important things you can do to ensure the success of your campaign. You will be able to launch a successful campaign with the assistance of a team, which can provide the necessary support and expertise. A crowdfunding team can assist you in the following ways:

Create a Campaign Pitch That Is Both Clear and Compelling Your team can provide you with feedback and support as you work to create a pitch for your campaign that is both clear and convincing.

Make a Game-Changing Video With the Help of Your Team Your team can assist you in making a game-changing video that highlights your project and engages your audience.

Your Team Can Assist You in Managing Your Campaign Your team is available to assist you in managing your campaign, which may include the creation of rewards and perks, the promotion of your campaign, and the engagement of your backers.

Offer Support and Resources: In order for you to launch a successful campaign, your team can offer the support and resources that you require, which may include expertise in areas such as marketing, finance, and law.

Recruiting Competent Individuals for the Positions Available

It is absolutely necessary for the success of your crowdfunding campaign to assemble a team composed of the appropriate members. The following are some considerations to make when selecting candidates for a position:

Determine Your Needs Determine the abilities and knowledge that you require for your campaign, such as marketing, design, or legal expertise, and write them down.

Look for Passion and Enthusiasm: When putting together your team, try to find people who are both passionate and enthusiastic about the project you are working on and the potential impact it could have.

Take Into Account Your Team Members' Experience and Expertise You should take into account the experience and expertise of the members of your team and select individuals who have the necessary skills to assist you in launching a successful campaign.

Select Team Members Who Possess Skills That Complement One Another Select team members who possess skills that complement one another and who are capable of working effectively together.

Maintain a Clear and Consistent Line of Communication: Maintain a clear and consistent line of communication with your team members regarding your expectations and goals, as well as provide them with regular feedback and support.

Establish a Solid Community: One of the most important things you can do for your team is to establish a solid community among its members and to encourage collaboration and cooperation.

Conclusion

Putting together a crowdsourcing team is one of the most important things you can do to ensure the success of your campaign. You can choose the right people for the job and launch a successful crowdfunding campaign if you first determine your needs, then look for people who are passionate and enthusiastic, then think about their experience and expertise, then pick skills that complement one another, then communicate clearly and consistently, and finally build a strong community. In the following chapter, we will discuss how to effectively manage and carry out your crowdsourcing campaign.

Chapter 7: The Power of Social Media: Maximizing Your Reach and Engagement

When it comes to promoting your crowdfunding campaign and engaging with your audience, one of the most effective tools is social media. In this chapter, we will discuss how to maximize your reach and engagement on social media platforms such as Facebook, Twitter, and Instagram.

Why Participation in Social Media is Essential for Crowdfunding Efforts

A successful crowdfunding campaign cannot function without the utilization of various social media platforms. It enables you to communicate with your backers and reach a larger audience overall, as well as to build a community of supporters. Kickstarter reports that campaigns that make active efforts to promote themselves on social media have a 2.4 times greater chance of being successful than campaigns that make no such efforts.

Getting the Most Out of Your Social Media Presence by Expanding Your Reach and Participation

It takes careful planning and precise execution in order to make the most of your reach and engagement on social media. The following advice will assist you in making the most of your presence across various social media platforms:

Select the Appropriate Platforms It is important to select social media platforms that are appropriate for your target audience and that are in line with the objectives of your campaign. Think about using social media sites such as Facebook, Twitter, Instagram, and LinkedIn.

Create a Social Media Strategy: Create a social media strategy for your campaign that is in line with the goals and objectives you have set for the campaign. Establish who your intended audience is as well as your messaging and content strategy.

Utilize Paid Advertising: If you want to increase the number of people who engage with your content and the amount of people who see it, you should think about using paid advertising on social media platforms. To get the most out of your advertising, tailor it to the demographics and interests of a specific audience.

Utilize Search Terms and Hashtags: Utilizing search terms and hashtags that are pertinent to your content will help it appear in search results and expose it to a larger audience.

Maintaining a Regular and Consistent Posting Schedule It is important to maintain a regular and consistent posting schedule across all of your social media channels in order to keep your audience interested and informed about the progress of your campaign.

Utilize Visuals and Video In order to create content that is more engaging and able to be shared, utilize visuals and video. Your content will be more likely to be shared if you include visuals, and they can also help your content stand out in the feeds of crowded social media platforms.

Engage with Your Audience: In order to engage with your audience, you should respond to comments, express gratitude to backers, and offer regular updates on the progress of your campaign. Inspire your audience to engage in the conversation by having them share your content and take part in it.

Monitor Your Social Media Performance, and Evaluate It Regularly Monitor your performance on social media, and evaluate it regularly.

Tracking engagement, reach, and conversion rates with the help of analytics tools will allow you to adjust your strategy appropriately.

Conclusion

When it comes to promoting your crowdfunding campaign and engaging with your audience, one of the most effective tools is social media. You can maximize your reach and engagement on social media and increase your chances of being successful by selecting the appropriate platforms, developing a social media strategy, utilizing paid advertising, utilizing hashtags and keywords, posting regularly and consistently, utilizing visuals and video, engaging with your audience, and monitoring and measuring the results of your efforts. In the following chapter, we will discuss how to effectively manage and carry out your crowdsourcing campaign.

Chapter 8: Navigating Legal Issues: Crowdfunding Regulations and Compliance

---

Various legal and regulatory requirements must be met in order for a crowdfunding campaign to be considered legitimate. When you start a crowdfunding campaign, there are certain legal considerations and regulations that you need to be aware of. We will go over those topics in this chapter.

The Current Regulatory Climate for Crowdfunding

The practice of crowdfunding is subject to a wide variety of legal and regulatory requirements, including those pertaining to consumer protection laws, tax laws, and securities laws. The following can be found in the regulatory landscape of crowdfunding:

The Jumpstart Our Business Startups (JOBS) Act was passed into law in 2012, and it established a regulatory framework for equity crowdfunding while also easing restrictions on the solicitation of investment from the general public.

Regulations Provided by the SEC The Securities and Exchange Commission (SEC) is the regulatory body in the United States that oversees crowdfunding campaigns. In accordance with SEC regulations, issuers are required to disclose certain information, investors must be protected, and fundraising caps must be adhered to.

Regulations at the State Level: In addition to being subject to federal regulations, crowdfunding campaigns are also subject to regulations at the state level, including requirements for registration and disclosure.

Tax Legislation: There is a possibility that crowdfunding campaigns will be subject to various tax regulations, such as income tax, sales tax, and property tax.

Compliance Requirements that Must Be Met by Crowdfunding Projects

It is absolutely necessary for the success of your crowdfunding campaign that you comply with all of the legal and regulatory requirements. The following is a list of compliance requirements that you should be aware of:

Disclosure of Securities If you are offering equity or ownership shares in your project, you are required to provide adequate disclosure to your investors. This disclosure must include financial statements, business plans, and a discussion of the risk factors associated with the endeavor.

Limits on Fundraising: Different types of crowdfunding campaigns, as well as the regulatory frameworks that govern them, may impose different caps on the amount of money that can be raised through those campaigns.

Anti-Fraud Requirements: Crowdfunding campaigns are required to comply with anti-fraud requirements, which include providing investors with accurate and complete information and avoiding statements that are misleading or deceptive.

Investor Protection: Campaigns that raise money through crowdfunding are required to offer investor protection, which includes terms and conditions that are easy to understand and completely transparent, investor education, and dispute resolution mechanisms.

Tax Compliance: Campaigns that use crowdfunding must ensure that they are in compliance with all applicable tax laws, such as those pertaining to income tax, sales tax, and property tax.

Conclusion

It is absolutely necessary for a successful crowdfunding campaign to have a solid understanding of the legal and regulatory requirements involved. You can ensure that your campaign complies with regulations and is successful by first gaining an understanding of the regulatory landscape of crowdfunding and then complying with regulatory requirements. These requirements include securities disclosure, fundraising limits, anti-fraud requirements, investor protection requirements, and tax compliance requirements. In the following chapter, we will discuss how to effectively manage and carry out your crowdsourcing campaign.

Chapter 9: Rewards and Perks: Creating Incentives for Backers

In any crowdfunding campaign, the rewards and perks offered to backers are an essential component. They offer a concrete reward to backers in exchange for their financial assistance, which encourages more people to contribute to your project. In this chapter, we will discuss how to create alluring rewards and perks for your backers to receive once the campaign has been successfully funded.

Various Forms of Rewards and Privileges

You can provide your backers with a wide variety of rewards and perks, some examples of which are as follows:

Early-bird Discounts: Provide reductions in pledge amounts to backers who contribute to your campaign at an earlier stage.

Offer Your Backers Exclusive Merchandise Give your backers the opportunity to purchase exclusive merchandise such as t-shirts, mugs, or posters.

Provide Unique Access Make available unique access to your project, such as access to the production behind the scenes or VIP experiences.

Items With Your Name On Them Give away items with your name on them, like copies of your book that have been signed by you or personalized thank-you notes.

Opportunities for Co-Creation: Provide your audience with opportunities for co-creation, such as the chance to name a character in your book or design a product feature.

Developing Intriguing Rewards and Benefits to Offer

Developing alluring benefits and privileges calls for careful deliberation and meticulous planning. The following are some suggestions for creating rewards and perks that will encourage people to contribute to your campaign:

Ensure That Your Rewards And Perks Are Relevant: Check to See That Your Rewards And Perks Are Relevant To Your Project And Are Aligned With The Interests Of Your Audience.

Think Outside the Box and Get Creative with Your Rewards and Perks Think outside the box when it comes to your rewards and perks. Think about providing one-of-a-kind or personalized products that stand out from the crowd.

Provide a Diverse Range of Rewards and Perks for Backers to Choose From Provide a diverse range of rewards and perks for backers to choose from, each with a unique price point.

Be Clear and Concise: Make sure that your rewards and perks are clear and concise, and provide all of the necessary details, including the anticipated delivery date.

Establish an Atmosphere of Exclusivity You can establish an atmosphere of exclusivity around your rewards and perks by limiting the number of items that are available or offering exclusive items to a select group of backers only.

Utilize Images and Visuals You can increase the allure of your benefits and advantages by showcasing them with the help of images and visuals.

Be Open: Be open and honest about the costs that are associated with your rewards and perks, including the fees for production, shipping, and handling.

Conclusion

In any crowdfunding campaign, the rewards and perks offered to backers are an essential component. You can incentivize your backers and increase the success of your campaign by providing rewards and perks that are pertinent, creative, and varied; being clear and concise; creating a sense of exclusivity; making use of images and visuals; and being transparent. In the following chapter, we will discuss how to effectively manage and carry out your crowdsourcing campaign.

Chapter 10: Setting Realistic Goals: Understanding Your Funding Needs

It is absolutely necessary for the success of a crowdfunding campaign to set goals that are attainable. In this chapter, we will discuss how to comprehend the funding requirements of your campaign and how to establish reasonable objectives for it.

Understanding Your Funding Needs

It is absolutely necessary to have a solid understanding of your funding requirements before you can set reasonable goals for your crowdfunding campaign. When evaluating your requirements for financial support, the following are some considerations to keep in mind:

Estimate the total cost of your project, including the costs of production, manufacturing, marketing, and distribution. This should include all of these costs.

Timeline: Establish the timeline for your project and calculate how much time will be required to finish it.

Consider the possibility of unanticipated expenses or delays, and factor those into your calculations regarding the amount of money you will need.

Stretch Goals: In order to prepare for unforeseen opportunities or difficulties, you might want to think about establishing some "stretch goals," also known as additional funding goals that go beyond your initial goal.

Establishing Objectives That Can Be Met

It is absolutely necessary for the success of your crowdfunding campaign to set goals that are attainable. The following are some suggestions for establishing goals that are attainable:

Be Specific: Establish objectives that are definite and quantifiable, such as a particular sum of money to be raised or a particular number of backers.

Be Realistic: In order to succeed, you must first establish goals that are reasonable and doable, taking into account the number of people who will be viewing your work.

Take Into Account Your Network When Establishing Your Goals, You Should Take Into Account Both the Size and Engagement of Your Network.

Make Use of Historical Data In order to inform your goal-setting process, make use of historical data obtained from previous crowdfunding campaigns.

Communicate Your Goals You should communicate your goals to your audience in a way that is both clear and consistent, and you should also provide them with regular updates on your progress.

Adjust as Necessary: Have a plan in place to adjust your goals as necessary in response to the development of your campaign and the comments and suggestions of your target audience.

Conclusion

It is absolutely necessary for the success of your crowdfunding campaign to set goals that are attainable. You will be able to increase the success of your campaign and set goals that are more realistic if you first understand your funding requirements, then establish goals that are specific and measurable, then be realistic, then take into account your network, then make use of historical data, then communicate your goals, and then adjust as necessary. In the following chapter, we will discuss how to effectively manage and carry out your crowdsourcing campaign.

Chapter 11: Pre-Launch Strategies: Building Buzz and Anticipation

It is critical to the success of your crowdfunding campaign that you generate excitement and anticipation before the campaign even begins. We will discuss pre-launch strategies in this chapter so that you can build buzz and anticipation for your campaign.

Pre-Launch Checklist

Before you start your crowdfunding campaign, there are a few essential steps you need to take in order to get everything ready and build up people's excitement for it, including the following:

Develop the strategy for your campaign: Create a campaign strategy that is not only comprehensible but also compelling. This strategy should include your goals, target audience, messaging, and content strategy.

Build Anticipation for Your Campaign by Creating a Landing Page You should create a landing page in order to build anticipation for your campaign and to collect the email addresses of potential backers.

Create a Customer Email List: By promoting your landing page across various channels, such as social media, blogs, and other websites, you can begin to compile an email list of potential donors.

Make Contact with Your Network: Make contact with your network, which should include your friends, family, and coworkers, and ask them to support your campaign and make the word known.

Collaboration with Influencers: If you want to promote your campaign and reach more people, you should collaborate with various online personalities, such as bloggers and other influencers.

Produce a Teaser Video: Produce a teaser video that not only highlights your project but also generates excitement for your campaign.

Build Buzz and Anticipation for Your Campaign by Promoting Your Teaser Video You can build buzz and anticipation for your campaign by promoting your teaser video through social media, email, and other channels.

Maintain Your Audience's Interest by Providing Regular Updates: Maintain your audience's interest in your project by providing regular updates on the progress of your campaign and by sharing content from behind the scenes.

Increasing Excitement and Anticipation

Creating a sense of excitement and anticipation for your crowdfunding campaign calls for an approach that is both strategic and focused. Here are some strategies that can be used to generate excitement and buzz:

Utilize Social Media: Make use of social media in order to generate excitement and anticipation for your campaign. You can keep your audience engaged and excited by providing them with updates, teasers, and other behind-the-scenes content.

In order to generate excitement and build anticipation for your campaign, you should consider throwing a launch event. This event could take the form of a party or a webinar.

Utilize Countdown Timers You can generate a sense of urgency and anticipation for the launch of your campaign by utilizing countdown timers on both your landing page and the social media channels you use.

Conduct a Contest: Conducting a contest or giving away prizes is a great way to generate buzz and encourage audience participation in spreading the word about your campaign.

Utilize Influencers: Forming strategic alliances with well-known people on social media or the internet can help you spread the word about your campaign and attract more people.

Provide Backers with Early-Bird Incentive Programs: Provide backers with early-bird incentive programs in order to encourage early support of your campaign and generate momentum.

Give Your Email List and Social Media Followers Access to Exclusive Content In order to build anticipation and excitement, give your email list and social media followers access to exclusive content such as behind-the-scenes access or sneak peeks.

Conclusion

It is critical to the success of your crowdfunding campaign that you generate excitement and anticipation before the campaign even begins. You can build buzz and anticipation for your campaign and increase the likelihood of it being successful if you follow a pre-launch checklist that includes developing your campaign strategy, building your email list, creating a teaser video, and promoting your campaign. Additionally, if you use pre-launch strategies such as social media, launch events, countdown timers, contests, influencers, early-bird incentive content, and exclusive content, you can build buzz and anticipation for your campaign. In the following chapter, we will discuss how to effectively manage and carry out your crowdsourcing campaign.

Chapter 12: Launch Day: Strategies for a Successful Campaign Launch

The day you launch your crowdfunding campaign is one of the most important days of the entire campaign. It's important to have a successful launch day so that you can generate momentum for your project and set the tone for the rest of your campaign. In this chapter, we will discuss strategies that will help you launch your campaign successfully.

Launch Day Checklist

Before you start your crowdfunding campaign, there are a few essential steps you need to take to get ready for the big day, including the following:

Complete Your Campaign Page Complete your campaign page by adding the finishing touches, such as your video, copy, and rewards, and double check that everything is understandable and enticing.

Check the Functionality of Your Campaign Page Conduct a check of your campaign page to ensure that it is error-free, fully functional, and responsive.

Make Sure Your Team Is Ready: Prepare your team to handle questions, comments, and inquiries on launch day.

Inform Your Network Share the news of your launch day with your network, which should include your email list, the people who follow you on social media, and any influential people you know, and encourage them to back your campaign.

Develop a Launch Strategy Develop a launch strategy that includes your goals, messaging, and outreach strategy for the day the product is launched.

Methods for Conducting an Effective and Profitable Marketing Campaign

The launch of a campaign requires careful planning and execution in order to be successful. The following are some strategies that can be used to launch a successful campaign:

Employ a Strategy Called a "Soft Launch" To employ a strategy known as a "soft launch," you must first launch your campaign to a limited number of backers, such as those on your email list or who follow you on social media, before you launch it to the general public. Before introducing it to a larger audience, you should do this so that you can test your campaign and generate early momentum for it.

Leverage Your Network: On the day that your campaign is launched, you should leverage your network by informing your email list, social media followers, and other influencers about the launch of your campaign and encouraging them to support and share your campaign.

Establish Realistic Objectives For the Beginning of Your Campaign Establish realistic objectives for the beginning of your campaign and communicate them clearly to your audience.

Provide Backers with Early-Bird Incentive Programs: Provide backers with early-bird incentive programs in order to encourage early support of your campaign and generate momentum.

Make Use of Paid Advertising: Make use of paid advertising on social media platforms in order to increase your reach and generate momentum on the day of your launch.

CROWDFUNDING SECRETS: A COMPREHENSIVE GUIDE TO SUCCESSFULLY FUNDING YOUR NEXT PROJECT

Maintain a Responsive Attitude: Maintain a responsive attitude toward questions, comments, and inquiries from your audience on the day of the launch as well as throughout the entirety of your campaign.

Maintain Your Audience's Interest by Providing Regular Updates: Maintain your audience's interest in your project by providing regular updates on the progress of your campaign and by sharing content from behind the scenes.

Conclusion

It is essential to the success of your crowdfunding campaign that the campaign itself be launched successfully. You can successfully launch your campaign and increase its chance of success by following a launch day checklist that includes finalizing your campaign page, testing your campaign page, preparing your team, alerting your network, and creating a launch plan, as well as by utilizing strategies for a successful campaign launch, such as a soft launch, leveraging your network, setting realistic goals, offering early-bird incentives, using paid advertising, being responsive, and providing regular updates. In the following chapter, we will discuss how to effectively manage and carry out your crowdsourcing campaign.

Chapter 13: Maintaining Momentum: Keeping Your Campaign Fresh and Engaging

It is critical to the success of your crowdfunding campaign that you keep the momentum going throughout the entire campaign. In this chapter, we will discuss various methods for maintaining the relevance and interest of your campaign.

Maintaining Momentum Checklist

Maintaining momentum throughout your crowdfunding campaign can be accomplished through the following key steps:

Establish Regular Milestones It is important to establish regular milestones for your campaign and communicate them to your audience in order to keep the momentum going and garner support.

Maintain Your Audience's Interest by Providing Regular Updates: Maintain your audience's interest in your project by providing regular updates on the progress of your campaign and by sharing content from behind the scenes.

Respond Promptly: In order to demonstrate your engagement and commitment to the project, you should respond promptly to any questions, comments, or inquiries that are submitted by your audience.

Conduct Contests and Give-Aways: Conducting contests and giving away prizes is a great way to generate buzz and encourage audience participation in spreading the word about your campaign.

Utilize Influencers: Forming strategic alliances with well-known people on social media or the internet can help you spread the word about your campaign and attract more people.

Make Available Limited-Time Incentives By making available limited-time incentives, you can generate a sense of urgency among backers and encourage them to contribute to your campaign.

Hold Live Events: Holding live events, such as question-and-answer sessions or webinars, is an excellent way to connect with your audience, as well as to keep your campaign feeling new and interesting to participants.

Maintaining the Vibrancy and Interest in Your Campaign

Keeping your campaign interesting and relevant requires creativity as well as active participation from your target audience. The following are some strategies that can be used to keep your campaign interesting and current:

Utilize Visual Content To demonstrate your work to an audience and maintain their interest, you should utilize visual content such as photographs and videos.

Tell a Story: One of the most effective ways to engage an audience and establish an emotional connection to a project is to tell a story.

Collaborate with Backers Collaborate with your backers by asking for their feedback, incorporating them into the creative process, and providing them with opportunities to participate in co-creation.

Give Access to Something Exclusive Give your email list subscribers and social media followers access to something exclusive, such as a sneak peek or access behind the scenes, in order to build up their anticipation and excitement.

Showcase Your Progress By showcasing your progress throughout the course of your campaign, you can demonstrate your dedication to the cause and earn the audience's trust.

Experiment with New Content: In order to maintain the vibrancy and interest of your campaign, try experimenting with new content types such as podcasts and infographics.

Engage Your Audience By using social media, email, and other channels to engage your audience, you can build relationships with them and ensure that your campaign is kept in the forefront of their minds.

Conclusion

It is critical to the success of your crowdfunding campaign that you keep the momentum going throughout the entire campaign. By adhering to a checklist for maintaining momentum, which includes setting regular milestones, providing regular updates, responding promptly, running contests and giveaways, leveraging influencers, offering limited-time incentives, and hosting live events, and by utilizing strategies to keep your campaign fresh and engaging, including the use of visual content, storytelling, collaborating with backers, providing exclusivity, showcasing progress, experimenting with new content, and engaging backers, you will be able to maintain momentum for your campaign. In the following chapter, we will discuss how to effectively manage and carry out your crowdsourcing campaign.

Chapter 14: Engaging Your Backers: Staying Connected and Building Community

The success of your crowdfunding campaign and the success of your project over the long term both depend on your ability to keep your backers interested and involved. In this chapter, we will discuss various methods for maintaining connections as well as constructing a community that is centered on your project.

Engaging Backers Checklist

The following are some important steps that should be taken in order to keep your backers interested and build a community around your project:

Maintain Frequent Communication: Maintaining frequent communication with your backers via email, social media, and other channels will keep them informed and engaged with your campaign.

Give Your Backers Access to Behind-the-Scenes Content Give your backers access to behind-the-scenes content such as production updates to keep them engaged and invested in the project you're working on.

Request Feedback One way to demonstrate your commitment to ensuring the happiness of your backers and to enhance your project is to request feedback from them.

Provide Opportunities for Co-Creation One way to get your backers involved in the creative process is to provide them with opportunities for co-creation. These could include naming a character in your book or designing a product feature.

You Should Give Your Backers Exclusive Content You should give your backers exclusive content as a reward for their support and to build loyalty to your brand. This could include early access to your project or sneak peeks at it.

Hold Live Events: Holding live events, such as question-and-answer sessions or webinars, is an excellent way to connect with your backers and develop a sense of community in relation to your project.

Express Your Gratitude Express your appreciation to your backers by thanking them both privately and publicly for their contribution.

Putting Down Roots in the Community

Engaging and working together with your backers is a necessary step in the process of building a community around your project. The following are some methods that can be used to construct a community:

Establish a Forum: Establish a discussion board or an online community in which contributors can communicate with one another and share their observations and experiences.

Facilitate Discussions, Request Feedback, and Solicit Ideas to Foster Backer Collaboration You can foster backer collaboration by facilitating discussions, requesting feedback, and soliciting ideas.

Share User-Generated Content One way to show your appreciation for your backers and build a sense of community is to share user-generated content such as fan art or testimonials.

Provide Incentives for Participation: Provide incentives for participation, such as special rewards or exclusive content, in order to encourage participation and build loyalty among audience members.

CROWDFUNDING SECRETS: A COMPREHENSIVE GUIDE TO SUCCESSFULLY FUNDING YOUR NEXT PROJECT

Meetups and other events should be hosted so that you can connect with your backers in person and build a stronger community. These events could include product demonstrations or launch parties.

Milestones Should Be Celebrated: Marking significant achievements, such as reaching a funding goal or introducing a new product feature, is a great way to express gratitude to your supporters and foster a sense of community in relation to your project.

Conclusion

It is essential to the success and growth of your project over the long term that you engage your backers and build a community around your project. By creating a forum, encouraging backer collaboration, providing behind-the-scenes content, soliciting feedback, offering co-creation opportunities, providing exclusive content, hosting live events, and saying thank you, and by following a checklist for engaging backers that includes communicating regularly, providing behind-the-scenes content, soliciting feedback, offering co-creation opportunities, providing exclusive content, hosting live events, and saying thank you, and by using strategies to build a community that includes hosting meetups and events, and celebrating milestone In the final chapter of this guide, we will provide a synopsis of the most important takeaways.

Chapter 15: Overcoming Obstacles: Common Challenges and How to Overcome Them

Crowdfunding campaigns frequently encounter difficulties and roadblocks, which can have an effect on how well they do. In this chapter, we will discuss common difficulties and the solutions to those difficulties.

Checklist of Frequently Encountered Obstacles

The following is a list of typical obstacles that may be encountered by crowdfunding campaigns:

Your campaign might have difficulty reaching a large audience, which could result in a smaller than expected amount of support.

Insufficient Backer Engagement It's possible that your backers will lose interest in your project as it progresses, which will result in decreased support.

Delays in Production: There is a possibility that your project will experience production delays, which will cause backers to become frustrated and disappointed.

Problems With Technology There is a possibility that your campaign page or the processing of payments will experience problems with technology, which will result in confusion and frustration among your backers.

Legal and Regulatory Concerns It's possible that your campaign will run into legal and regulatory problems, such as failing to comply with securities laws or infringing on someone else's intellectual property.

How to Thrive Despite Difficulties

The following are some strategies that can be used to overcome typical obstacles in crowdfunding campaigns:

Limited Reach: Make use of social media and other online channels in order to broaden your campaign's audience and increase the number of people who are exposed to it. If you want more people to see your content, you should form partnerships with influencers and other online personalities.

Insufficient Backer Engagement It is important to keep your backers engaged and invested in your project by providing them with regular updates and content that goes behind the scenes. Request comments and incorporate your backers into the design process to demonstrate your dedication to ensuring they are happy with the end result.

Delays in Production: If there are any delays in production, you need to be open and honest about them, and you also need to provide regular updates on your progress. Maintain open lines of communication with your contributors and demonstrate that you are dedicated to delivering a product of the highest possible standard.

Difficulties of a Technical Nature You should have a backup plan ready in case there are any difficulties of a technical nature, and you should be receptive to questions and concerns raised by your backers. Maintain communication with your backers and demonstrate that you are committed to finding solutions to any problems that may arise.

Seek the advice of an attorney and make sure that you are in compliance with all of the laws and regulations that are relevant to the situation.

Maintain open communication with your backers about any potential legal or regulatory hurdles, and demonstrate that you are committed to overcoming those hurdles.

Conclusion

It's possible for crowdfunding campaigns to face a variety of challenges and roadblocks, any one of which can have an effect on how well they do. You can overcome these obstacles and increase the likelihood of your campaign being successful if you are proactive and transparent, if you communicate frequently with your backers, if you provide content that is behind-the-scenes and early access, if you involve your backers in the creative process, if you have a backup plan in case there are technical difficulties, and if you seek legal advice and comply with regulations.

Chapter 16: Managing Finances: Budgeting and Fulfillment Strategies

The management of your finances is absolutely necessary if you want your crowdfunding campaign as well as your project to be successful in the long run. In this chapter, we will discuss strategies for managing your finances, specifically budgeting and fulfilling obligations.

Budgeting Checklist

The following are some important steps to take when developing a budget for your crowdfunding campaign:

Determine Your Funding Goal Determine your funding goal by tallying up the costs of your project and the amount of money that will be required.

Determine Your Fundraising Goal by Computing Your Expenses Your fundraising goal can be determined by computing all of your expenses, including the costs of production, marketing, and shipping.

Establish Realistic Goals Establish reasonable goals that are in line with both your financial resources and your capacity for production.

Prepare for Unexpected Costs and Delays in Production One way to prepare for unforeseen costs and delays in production is to set aside funds specifically for use in unexpected circumstances.

Utilize Budgeting Tools To keep tabs on your spending and ensure that you don't go over your allotted spending money, make use of budgeting tools such as spreadsheets and software.

Fulfillment Checklist

The following are some of the most important steps to take when managing fulfillment for your crowdsourcing campaign:

Prepare for Fulfillment To prepare for fulfillment, you will need to determine your shipping costs, the type of packaging you will require, and your production timeline.

Discuss Your Fulfillment Plans with Your Backers Discuss your fulfillment plans with your backers, including estimated delivery dates and any potential delays.

Make Use of a Fulfillment Service If you want your shipping and fulfillment needs to be taken care of, you should make use of a fulfillment service, such as a third-party logistics provider.

Establish Quality Control As a Priority One of your top priorities should be establishing quality control. One way to do this is to inspect your products and their packaging to ensure that they meet both your standards and the standards of your backers.

Maintain Accurate Records: Be sure to maintain accurate records of your order fulfillment process, including any tracking numbers for shipments and customer service inquiries.

Conclusion

The management of your finances is absolutely necessary if you want your crowdfunding campaign as well as your project to be successful in the long run. You will be able to effectively manage your finances and ensure the success of your crowdfunding campaign and project if you follow a budgeting checklist that includes determining your funding goal, calculating your expenses, setting realistic rewards, planning for contingencies, and using budgeting tools. Additionally, if you follow a fulfillment checklist that includes planning for fulfillment, communicating with your backers, using a fulfillment service, prioritizing quality control, and keeping records, you will be able to follow a fulfillment checklist that includes these items.

Chapter 17: The Aftermath: Post-Campaign Strategies for Success

Your crowdfunding campaign is not finished once the allotted time for donations has passed. In point of fact, the period of time after the conclusion of your campaign is just as important to the overall success of the project you are working on. After the campaign is over, we will discuss successful post-campaign strategies in this chapter.

Checklist for After the Campaign

Following are some important steps you should take to ensure the success of your crowdfunding campaign:

Your Obligations: You are obligated to fulfill your obligations to your backers, which include delivering rewards promptly and keeping them informed of any potential delays.

Thank You to Your Supporters: Thank your backers both privately and publicly for their contribution, as this will demonstrate your appreciation to them.

Continue to Communicate With Your Backers After the Campaign Is Over After the campaign is over, continue to communicate with your backers, providing them with updates on your project and engaging them in the post-campaign process.

Make Use of the Momentum of Your Campaign to Expand Your Reach Make use of the momentum of your campaign to continue promoting your project to a wider audience and expand your reach.

Think About Future Campaigns You should think about running additional crowdfunding campaigns in the future in order to fund additional stages of your project or to start new projects.

Success Strategies for After the Campaign Is Over

The following are some post-campaign strategies for achieving success:

Inform Your Backers: It is important that you continue to keep your backers informed about the status of your project as well as any new developments that may occur after the campaign has ended. Give them regular updates and content from behind the scenes to keep them interested in and invested in the project you're working on.

Additional Rewards: As a way to thank your backers for their support and cultivate their loyalty to your brand, consider providing them with either additional rewards or exclusive content.

Continue to Engage Your Backers You should continue to build relationships with your backers by engaging them through social media, email, and other channels. This will help keep your project at the forefront of their minds.

Increase the Size of Your Network One way to increase the size of your network is to form partnerships with other online personalities and influencers in order to promote your project to a larger audience.

Request and Use Feedback Request and use feedback from your backers to help you improve your project and create a better product.

Conclusion

The results of your crowdfunding campaign will have a significant impact on the accomplishment of your project in the long run. After the conclusion of your crowdfunding campaign, you can ensure the continued success of your project by adhering to a post-campaign checklist and making use of strategies for post-campaign success. Some of these strategies include keeping your backers informed, offering additional rewards, continuing to engage your backers, expanding your network, and seeking feedback. Other strategies include fulfilling your promises, expressing gratitude to your backers, continuing communication, expanding your reach, and considering future campaigns.

Chapter 18: Going Global: Expanding Your Reach Beyond Your Borders

The practice of crowdfunding has evolved into a widespread phenomenon, with backers coming from all over the world to support campaigns located in a variety of countries. In this chapter, we will discuss various strategies that can help you extend the reach of your crowdfunding campaign beyond the boundaries of your country and into the international arena.

Going Global Checklist

The following are some of the most important steps to take in order to make your crowdfunding campaign global:

Conduct Research on International Markets It is important to conduct research on international markets in order to determine the nations in which there is a demand for your good or service.

Translate Your Content In order to communicate with a larger number of people, you should translate the content of your campaign page as well as any other relevant content.

Take into Account the Shipping Options One should take into account the various shipping options as well as the associated costs for international backers. These options include partnering with local fulfillment services or using international shipping carriers.

Be Aware of the Differences in Culture When promoting your campaign, you should be aware of the differences in culture and consider adapting your messaging to suit the various audiences you will be reaching.

Comply with International Laws and Regulations It is important to ensure that the fulfillment process runs smoothly by complying with international laws and regulations. This includes paying any applicable taxes and customs duties.

Methods for Expanding Internationally

The following are some strategies that can help you take your crowdfunding campaign to a global level:

Collaborate with Local Influencers: Collaborating with local influencers or online personalities in different countries can help you reach a larger audience and promote your campaign.

Utilize Social Media: Make use of social media to target specific audiences in various countries and engage with them in the language that is native to that country.

Participate in International Events By participating in international events, such as trade shows or conferences, you will have the opportunity to network with potential investors and partners in a variety of countries.

Provide Backers in Different Countries with Country-Specific Rewards and Incentives Provide backers in various countries with rewards and incentives that are specific to their country.

Utilize Localization Tools: Utilize localization tools, such as translation software or international shipping calculators, to make the process of fulfilling pledges easier for backers located in other countries.

Conclusion

When you take your crowdfunding campaign beyond your country's borders and into the international sphere, you can create new openings for expansion and achievement in your business. You can broaden your reach and increase sales by adhering to a checklist for going global, which includes things like researching international markets, translating your content, thinking about shipping options, being aware of cultural differences, and complying with international laws and regulations, and by employing strategies for going global, which include partnering with local influencers, using social media, attending international events, offering country-specific rewards, and leveraging localization tools.

Chapter 19: Success Stories: Inspiring Tales of Crowdfunding Triumph

Crowdfunding has made it possible for entrepreneurs, creators, and innovators to realize their visions and bring their ideas to fruition. In this chapter, we will discuss some motivational success stories that have been achieved through the use of crowdfunding.

First in a series of successes: the Oculus Rift

Oculus Rift is a piece of hardware that allows users to experience virtual reality. It was initially presented on Kickstarter in the year 2012. The campaign was able to raise over $2.4 million, which was a significant increase from its original goal of $250,000. Because of how well the campaign did, Facebook was able to purchase Oculus VR for $2 billion in 2014. This took place in 2014.

Pebble Time — the Second Successful Venture

The Pebble Time is a smartwatch that was initially presented on the crowdfunding platform Kickstarter in the year 2015. The campaign was successful, garnering more than $20 million in donations, making it the most funded project on Kickstarter at the time. Fitbit ultimately decided to purchase Pebble in the year 2016.

Exploding Kittens is the Third Successful Story.

The card game known as Exploding Kittens made its debut on the crowdfunding platform Kickstarter in the year 2015. The campaign was successful in raising more than 8 million dollars, making it the most funded game in the history of Kickstarter. Due to the overwhelming success of the campaign, a mobile application as well as a product line were both developed.

Success Story Number Four: The Chilliest Cooler

The Coolest Cooler is a versatile cooler that was initially presented on the crowdfunding platform Kickstarter in the year 2014. The campaign was successful in raising over $13 million, which placed it in the position of the second most funded project on Kickstarter at the time. The team behind Coolest Cooler eventually fulfilled all orders and continued to expand their product line, despite the fact that production had been delayed due to challenges and obstacles.

Reading Rainbow is the topic of the fifth success story.

The educational program known as Reading Rainbow made its debut on the crowdfunding platform Kickstarter in the year 2014. The fundraising effort brought in over $5 million, far exceeding the campaign's initial goal of $1 million. A new Reading Rainbow app was developed as a direct result of the success of the campaign, which also resulted in the program being brought into more classrooms across the United States.

These examples serve as evidence of the efficacy of crowdfunding as a method for bringing previously unrealized creative endeavors to fruition and for facilitating the development of communities of backers who are committed to seeing projects through to fruition. Entrepreneurs and creatives have been able to conquer challenges and make their dreams come true by harnessing the power of crowdfunding.

Conclusion

Crowdfunding has proven to be a revolutionary tool for business owners, creatives, and other innovators all over the world. The ability of crowdfunding to bring innovative ideas to life and to create new opportunities for success is demonstrated by the successes of projects such as Oculus Rift, Pebble Time, Exploding Kittens, Coolest Cooler, and Reading Rainbow. These crowdfunding campaigns' successes should serve as a source of motivation for you as you begin your own campaign; at the same time, you should have faith in the potential of your own idea to change the world.

Chapter 20: The Future of Crowdfunding: Trends and Predictions for the Next Decade

Since its inception, crowdfunding has come a long way, and it continues to evolve and shape the landscape of entrepreneurship and innovation in new and interesting ways. In this chapter, we will discuss the trends that have been observed and the predictions that have been made regarding the future of crowdfunding in the next ten years.

Recent Developments in Crowdfunding

The following are some trends in crowdfunding that are influencing the industry's trajectory going forward:

Equity crowdfunding: Equity crowdfunding, in which investors can buy a stake in a company in exchange for funding, is becoming increasingly popular, particularly with the passage of new laws and regulations in countries all over the world. Equity crowdfunding allows investors to buy a stake in a company for the same amount of funding that they put in.

Blockchain Technology and Cryptocurrency: The blockchain technology and cryptocurrency are currently being integrated into crowdfunding platforms. This will allow backers to use digital currency to fund projects and invest in startups.

Community-Driven Campaigns: As creators strive to cultivate long-term relationships and brand loyalty with their audience, a trend that is becoming increasingly prevalent is the use of community-driven campaigns. These campaigns put the wants, needs, and interests of backers and customers first.

Artificial Intelligence and Machine Learning: Both artificial intelligence and machine learning are currently being incorporated into crowdfunding platforms in order to provide backers and creators with data-driven insights and personalized recommendations.

Crowdfunding is increasingly being used to support projects and startups that have a social impact or that focus on sustainability. This trend is a reflection of the growing demand for purpose-driven investing and entrepreneurship.

Forecasts for the Development of the Crowdfunding Industry

The following are some forecasts regarding the development of crowdsourcing in the coming decade:

Crowdfunding is expected to continue its rapid growth, which is being driven by new technologies and the rising popularity of community-driven and purpose-driven initiatives. This growth is expected to continue for the foreseeable future.

Increased Regulation It is likely that regulators will impose more stringent regulations on crowdfunding as the practice continues to gain mainstream acceptance. These regulations are intended to protect investors and ensure compliance with securities laws.

Crowdfunding is likely to converge with traditional finance as established financial institutions and venture capital firms seek to participate in the crowdfunding market. This is due to the fact that traditional finance has been around for much longer than crowdfunding.

Expansion into Developing Countries It is anticipated that crowdfunding will expand into developing countries, thereby providing new opportunities for business owners and creatives to gain access to funding and resources.

Increased Emphasis on Social Impact It is anticipated that crowdfunding will place an increased emphasis on social impact and sustainability, which will reflect the growing demand for purpose-driven investing and entrepreneurialism.

Conclusion

The future of crowdfunding looks promising, with continued growth, the introduction of new technologies, and an emphasis on community- and mission-driven initiatives. It is essential for creators and investors to stay current with the most recent trends and predictions in order to capitalize on the opportunities and challenges presented by the industry. As crowdfunding continues to develop and change the landscape of entrepreneurship and innovation, it is essential that creators and investors stay current. Whether you are a seasoned crowdfunding veteran or are just getting started, the future of crowdfunding offers exciting new possibilities for bringing innovative ideas to life and making a difference in the world. Whether you are just getting started or are a seasoned crowdfunding veteran, the future of crowdfunding offers exciting new possibilities.

Also by B. Vincent

Affiliate Marketing
Affiliate Marketing
Affiliate Marketing

Standalone
Business Employee Discipline
Affiliate Recruiting
Business Layoffs & Firings
Business and Entrepreneur Guide
Business Remote Workforce
Career Transition
Project Management
Precision Targeting
Professional Development
Strategic Planning
Content Marketing
Imminent List Building
Getting Past GateKeepers
Banner Ads
Bookkeeping
Bridge Pages
Business Acquisition

Business Bogging
Business Communication Course
Marketing Automation
Better Meetings
Business Conflict Resolution
Business Culture Course
Conversion Optimization
Creative Solutions
Employee Recruitment
Startup Capital
Employee Incentives
Employee Mentoring
Followership
Servant Leadership
Human Resources
Team Building
Freelancing
Funnel Building
Geo Targeting
Goal Setting
Immanent List Building
Lead Generation
Leadership Course
Leadership Transition
Leadership vs Management
LinkedIn Ads
LinkedIn Marketing
Messenger Marketing
New Management
Newsfeed Ads
Search Ads
Online Learning
Sales Webinars

Side Hustles
Split Testing
Twitter Timeline Advertising
Earning Additional Income Through Side Hustles: Begin Earning Money Immediately
Making a Living Through Blogging: Earn Money Working From Home
Create Bonuses for Affiliate Marketing: Your Success Is Encompassed by Your Bonuses
Internet Marketing Success: The Most Effective Traffic-Driving Strategies
JV Recruiting: Joint Ventures Partnerships and Affiliates
Secrets to List Building
Step-by-Step Facebook Marketing: Discover How To Create A Strategy That Will Help You Grow Your Business
Banner Advertising: Traffic Can Be Boosted by Banner Ads
Affiliate Marketing
Improve Your Marketing Strategy with Internet Marketing
Outsourcing Helps You Save Time and Money
Choosing the Right Content and Marketing for Social Media
Make Products That Will Sell
Launching a Product for Affiliate Marketing
Pinterest as a Marketing Tool
Banner Blitz: Mastering the Art of Advertising with Eye-Catching Banners
Beyond Commissions: Maximizing Affiliate Profits with Creative Bonus Strategies
Retargeting Mastery: Winning Sales with Online Strategies
Power Partnerships: Mastering the Art of Business Growth Through Partnership Recruiting
The List Advantage: Unlocking the Power of List Building for Marketing Success
Capital Catalyst: The Essential Guide to Raising Funds for Your Business

Mobile Mastery: The Ultimate Guide to Successful Mobile Marketing Campaigns

Crowdfunding Secrets: A Comprehensive Guide to Successfully Funding Your Next Project

About the Publisher

Accepting manuscripts in the most categories. We love to help people get their words available to the world.

Revival Waves of Glory focus is to provide more options to be published. We do traditional paperbacks, hardcovers, audio books and ebooks all over the world. A traditional royalty-based publisher that offers self-publishing options, Revival Waves provides a very author friendly and transparent publishing process, with President Bill Vincent involved in the full process of your book. Send us your manuscript and we will contact you as soon as possible.

Contact: Bill Vincent at rwgpublishing@yahoo.com

www.ingramcontent.com/pod-product-compliance
Lightning Source LLC
LaVergne TN
LVHW011732060526
838200LV00051B/3145